The Woodland Elves
Little Letters and Limericks
Filled With Love

Shary Williamson
Illustrated by Jay Johnston

The Woodland Elves, LLC
Marion, Ohio

Copyrighted Material

The Woodland Elves: LITTLE LETTERS and LIMERICKS Filled With Love

Copyright © 2021 by The Woodland Elves, LLC. All Rights Reserved.

No part of this publication may be reproduced, stored in a retrieval system or transmitted, in any form or by any means—electronic, mechanical, photocopying, recording or otherwise—without prior written permission from the publisher, except for the inclusion of brief quotations in a review.

For information about this title or to order other books and/or electronic media, contact the publisher:

The Woodland Elves, LLC

www.thewoodlandelves.com

ISBN: 978-0-9903849-7-7

Library of Congress Catalog Number: 2021917692

Printed in the United States of America

10 9 8 7 6 5 4 3 2 1

Cover and interior design by Michele DeFilippo/1106 Design (www.1106design.com)

Cover art by Jay Johnston © The Woodland Elves, LLC

To purchase any of the following books or to inquire about presentations for your school or organization contact:

The Woodland Elves, Shary Williamson

PH. 740-225-8391   shary@roadrunner.com

Facebook: Shary Williamson   www.thewoodlandelves.com

The following books, CDs are available:

THE WOODLAND ELVES

The Woodland Elves, THE SECRET IN THE FOREST

The Woodland Elves, BURIED TREASURE

The Woodland Elves, A MAGICAL TALE OF WINTER

The Woodland Elves, FANTASY IN THE FOREST

The Woodland Elves, LITTLE LETTERS and LIMERICKS Filled With Love

This book is dedicated to everyone who loves to laugh. Well, since we **ALL** love to laugh, then this book is dedicated to <u>**YOU**</u>. Humor brings us together and this is surely a time when we all need to stick together and find JOY in the little things. Laughter is infectious, so go ahead and start reading and laughing.

We had such fun writing this so that YOU would have fun reading it. All of the elf tales are filled with an irrestible fun factor. This book is no different, so please enjoy every page and then help us spread the JOY around the world. By the way, you can *put your own name* on the line at the top of each letter. And you can also listen to Shary reading the book to you by just scanning the QR code on each page. It's easy and adds a new dimension.

We believe LAUGHTER and FUN are part of the reason *The Woodland Elves'* **books are now in 92 countries and all 7 continents.**

Thank you being part of the elfin family. Having fun can be the spark that connects and inspires us to be part of something positive. Sometimes, it just takes a little fun to bring us together. WE LOVE YOU.

Pg 4–5 Geese	Pg 26–27 Worms
Pg 6–7 Friends	Pg 28–29 Ants
Pg 8–9 Dollar	Pg 30–31 Bubbles
Pg 10–11 Marshmallow	Pg 32–33 Time Capsule
Pg 12–13 Watermelon	Pg 34–35 Shadow
Pg 14–15 Mud	Pg 36–37 Hammock
Pg 16–17 Four leaf clover	Pg 38–39 Hill
Pg 18–19 Shell	Pg 40–41 Clouds
Pg 20–21 Picnic	Pg 42–43 Letter
Pg 22–23 Spider	Pg 44–45 Gold
Pg 24–25 Dandelion	Pg 46–47 Picture

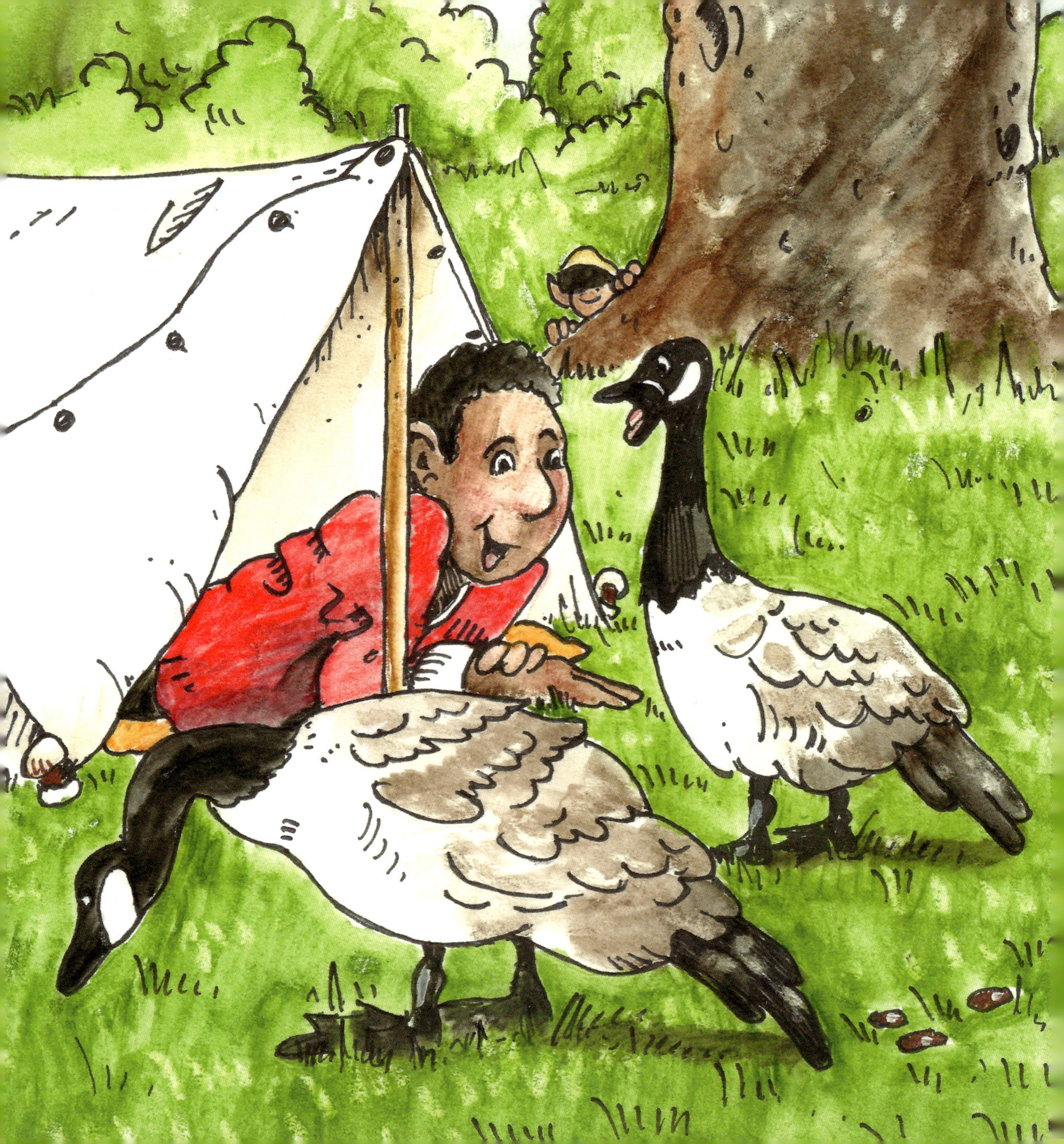

Dear _____,

I saw you having fun while you were camping out. Loud honking outside your tent woke you up. But it wasn't cars. It was geese. They are social birds. They like to have lots of their goose friends around them. They are so beautiful and look so peaceful. But here's my advice to you. Don't follow them too closely.

Here is a little poem I made up for you.

I must share with you some sad news

Geese can leave behind little clues

That though they are pretty

It's still such a pity

You'll prob'ly get poop on your shoes

I love you.

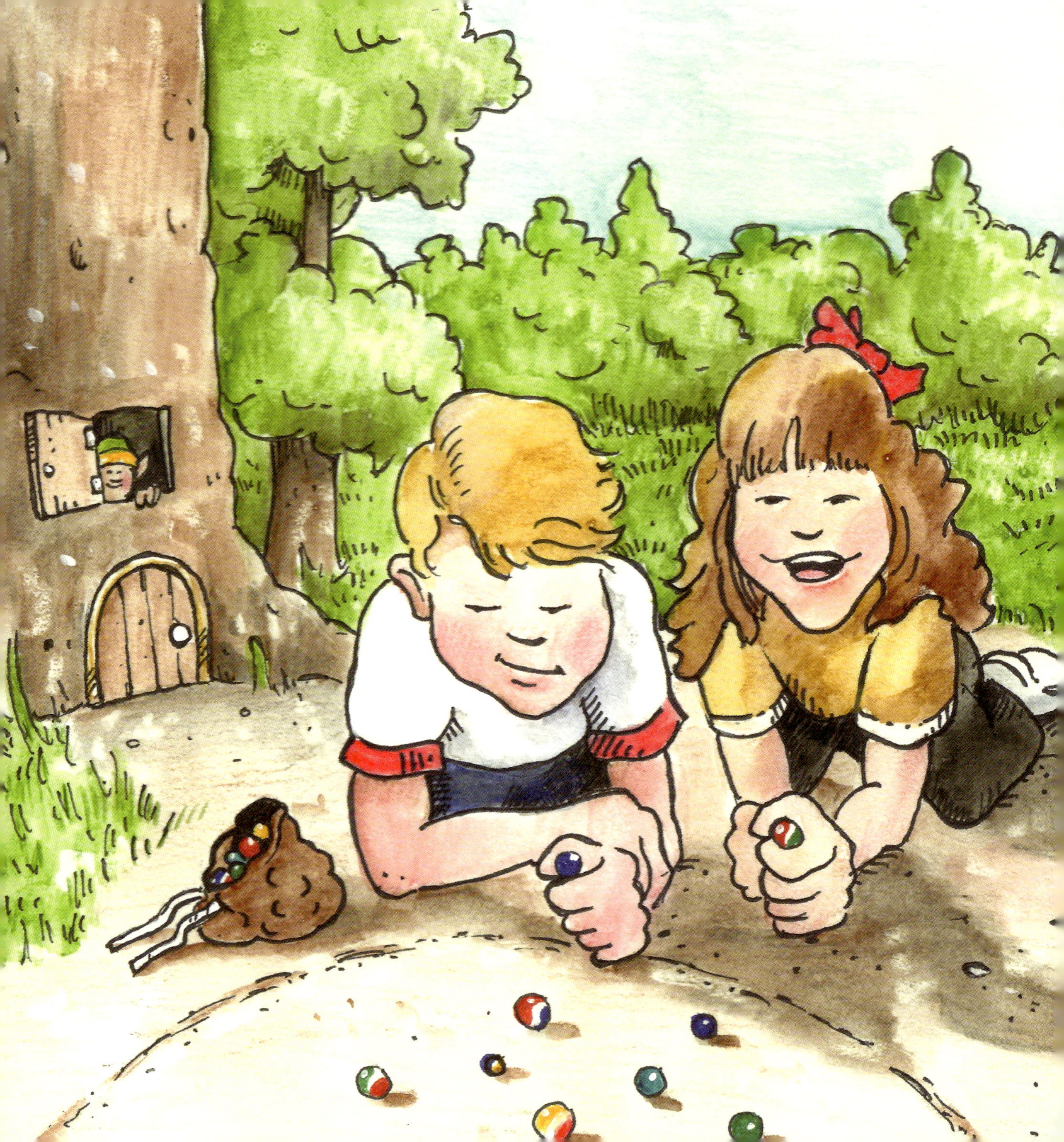

Dear _____,

I have watched you and your friend play marbles together many times. You always laugh and have so much fun. You take turns. Sometimes you talk. Sometimes you listen. Sometimes you trade your favorite marbles. You are always kind to each other. I like that. Being kind is so important.

Here is a little poem I made up for you.

I love that it's just "you and me"

I think that's the way it should be

There's no need to pretend

'Cause you'll be my best friend

Until we're one hundred and three

I love you.

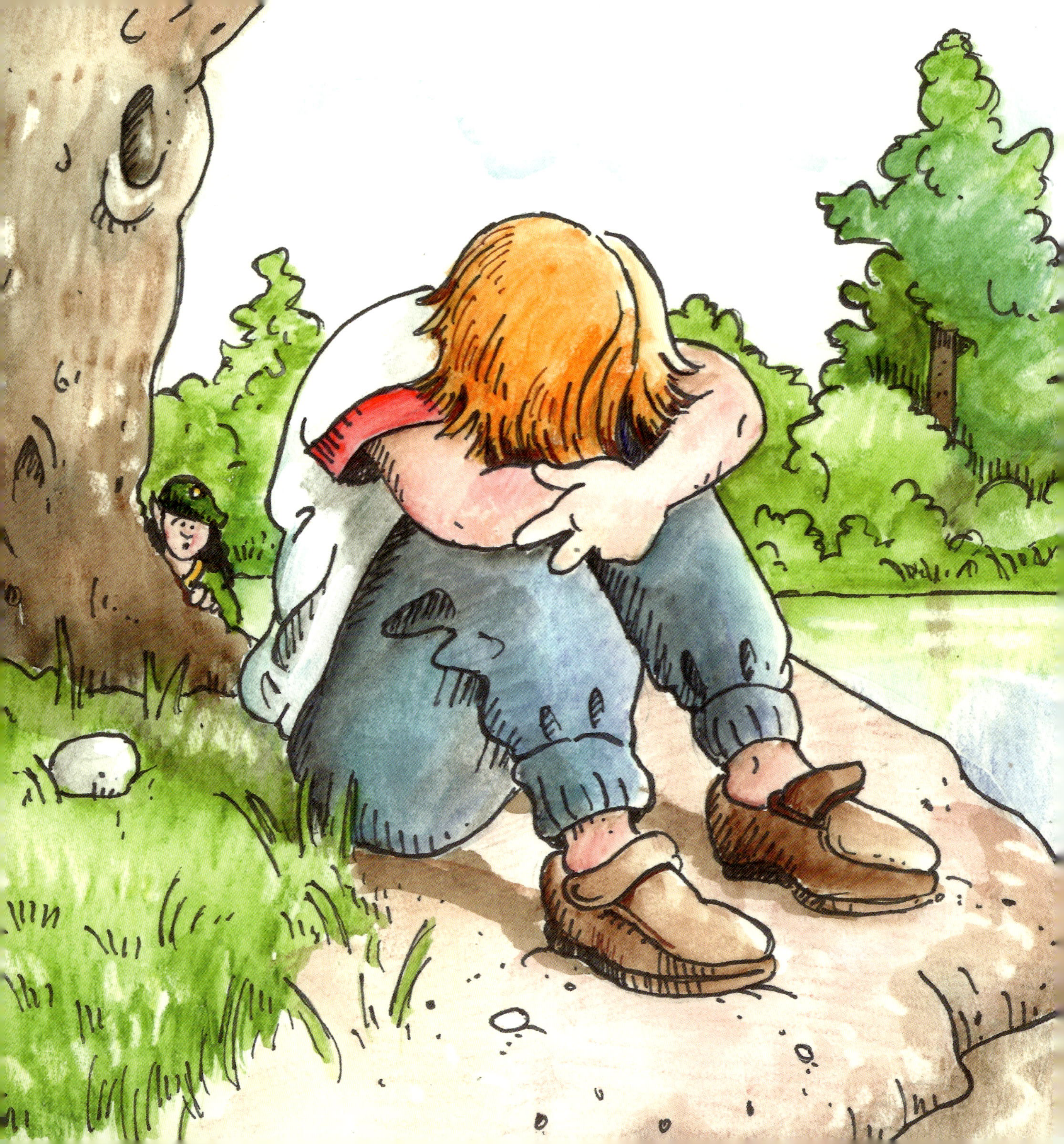

Dear _____,

I heard you talking to yourself the other day. You were not happy with the way that you looked. We ALL feel that way from time to time. Elves wish we could be taller. We wish our ears could be smaller. Ears? Taller? But that's a silly way to think because I am perfect just the way that I am and SO ARE YOU.

Here is a little poem I made up for you.

I'd pay somebody a dollar

If they could make my ears smaller

Then it comes to my mind

I surely would find

That I still wouldn't be any taller

I love you.

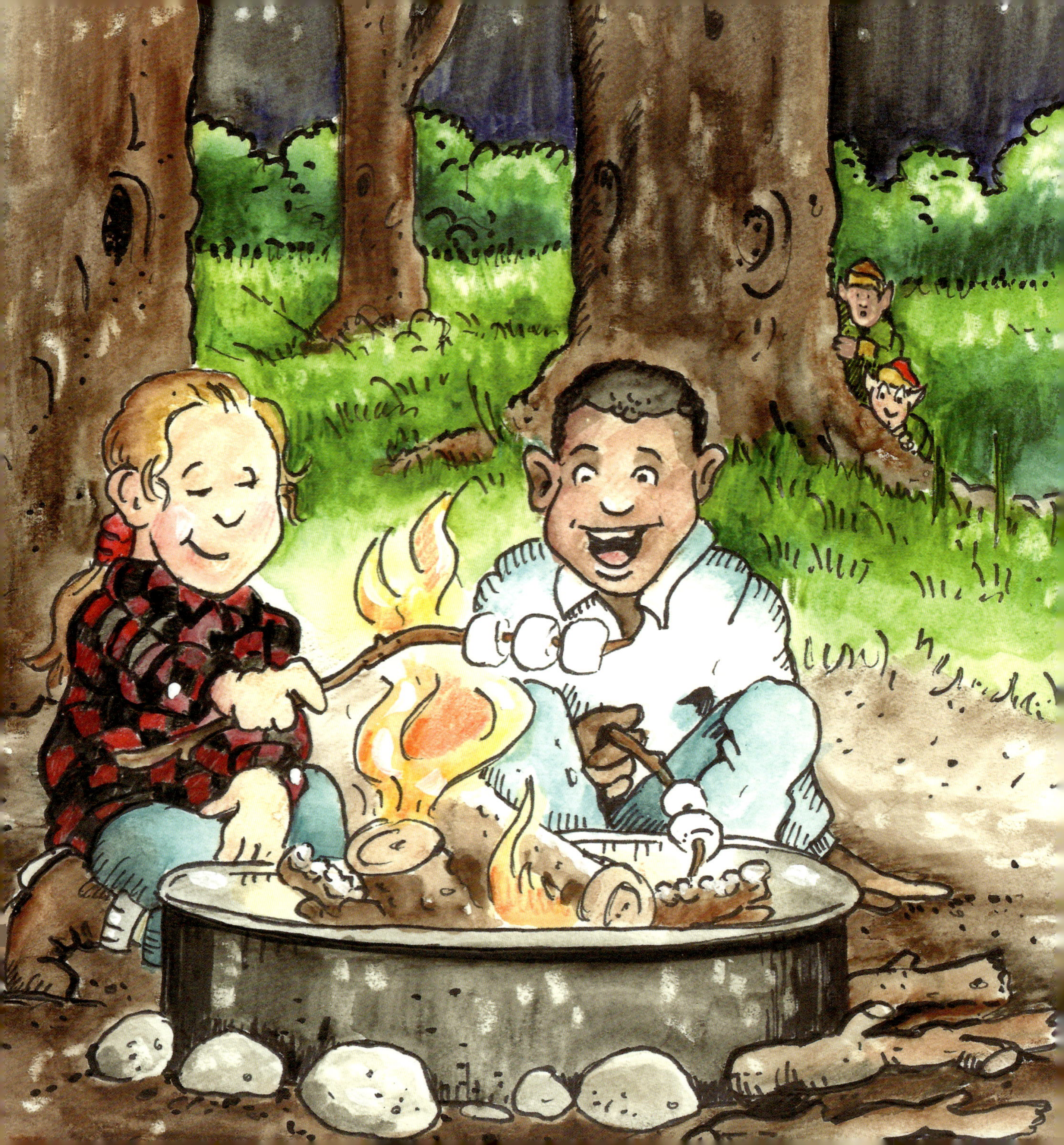

Dear _____,

I loved watching you roast marshmallows over the fire. Even though we love to nibble on them, to us, marshmallows are very big. They look like they would be fun for us to use as trampolines. But, if we jumped too high or hard, you'd never see us again because we would disappear in the sweet gooey middle.

Here is a little poem I made up for you.

A marshmallow on a long stick

Puffs up and gets black really quick

The flames from the fire

Grow higher and higher

If I ate too much, I'd get sick

I love you.

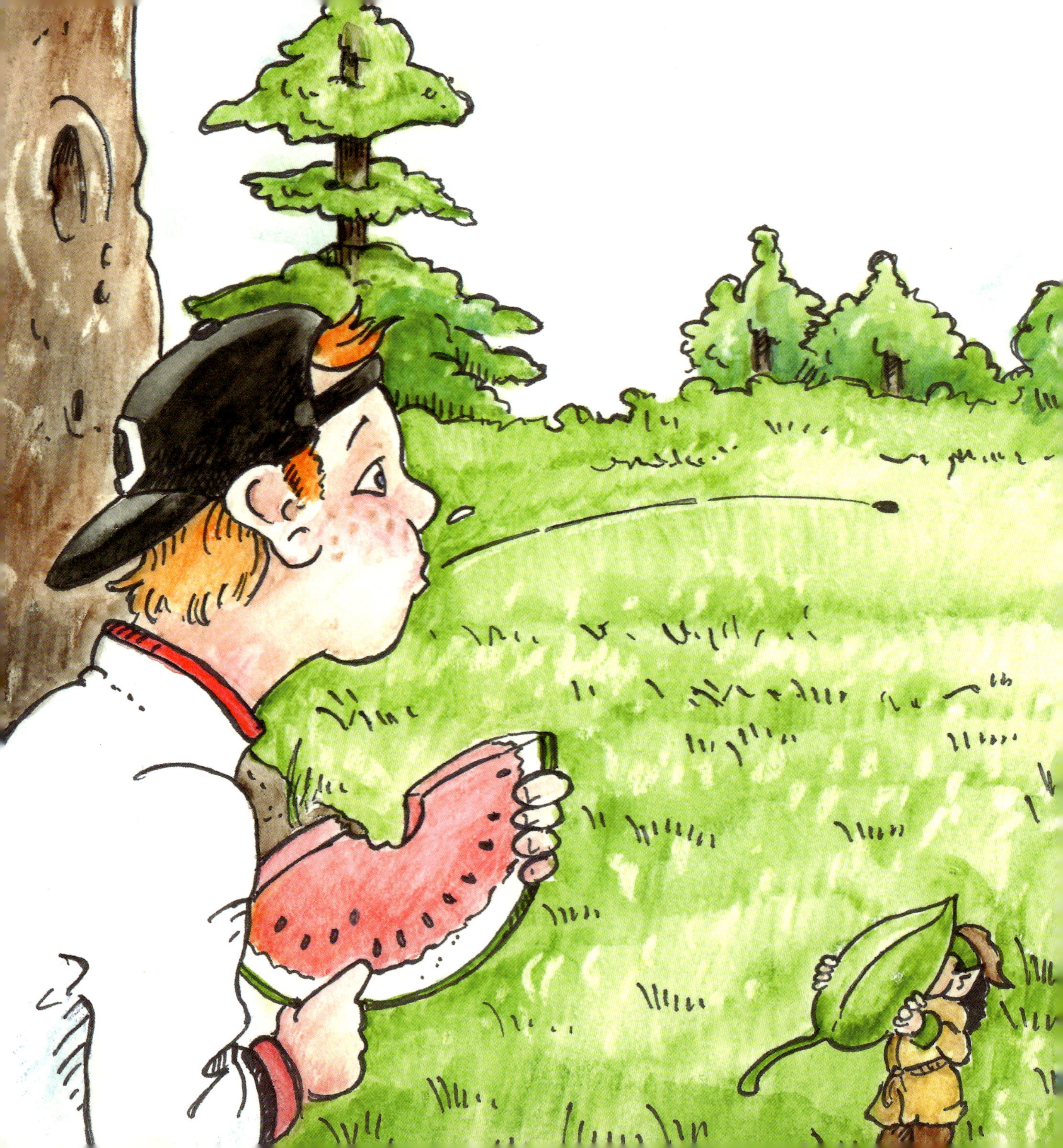

Dear _____,

I watched you spitting watermelon seeds today. I buried my head in a leaf so you would not hear me laughing. You took a deep breath and then blew as hard as you could. The seed flew off of the tip of your tongue. I laughed until one of your seeds bounced off of my head. You better work on your aim. Ha ha

Here is a little poem I made up for you.

Spitting seeds is really such fun

And makes all the other kids run

If it lands on a head

You have something to dread

And in that case, you're probably done

I love you.

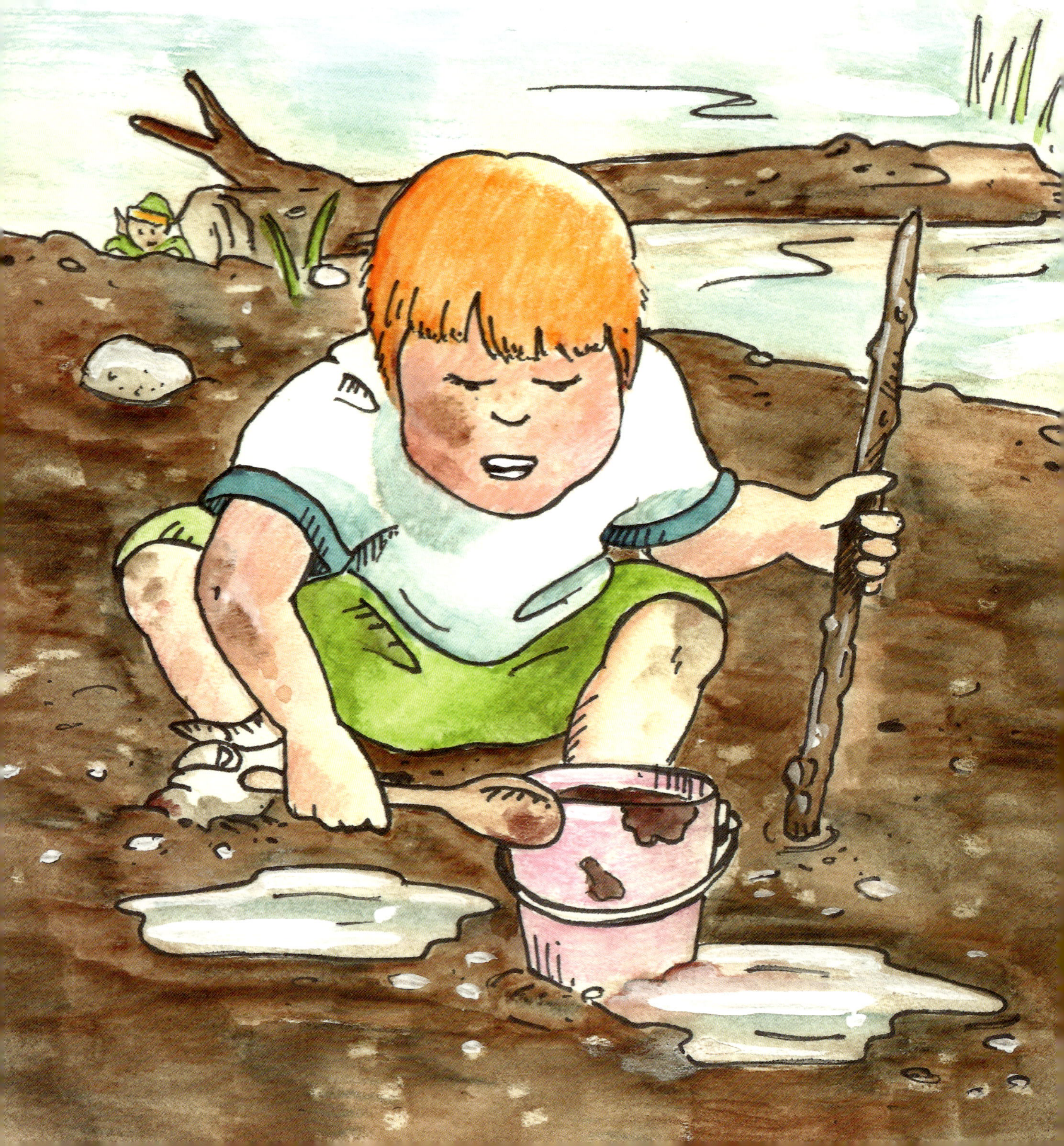

Dear _____,

I loved seeing you play in the dirt today. I couldn't tell exactly what you were creating, but you were having fun whipping up mud in your pail. You were stirring and mixing with a big stick that looked like a magic wand. I thought maybe you were creating a secret sauce. I won't share your secret. I promise.

Here's a little poem I made up for you.

Your pail of mud looked so yummy

And I know you are no dummy

As you stirred and you mixed

With your magical sticks

That stew was not meant for your tummy

I love you.

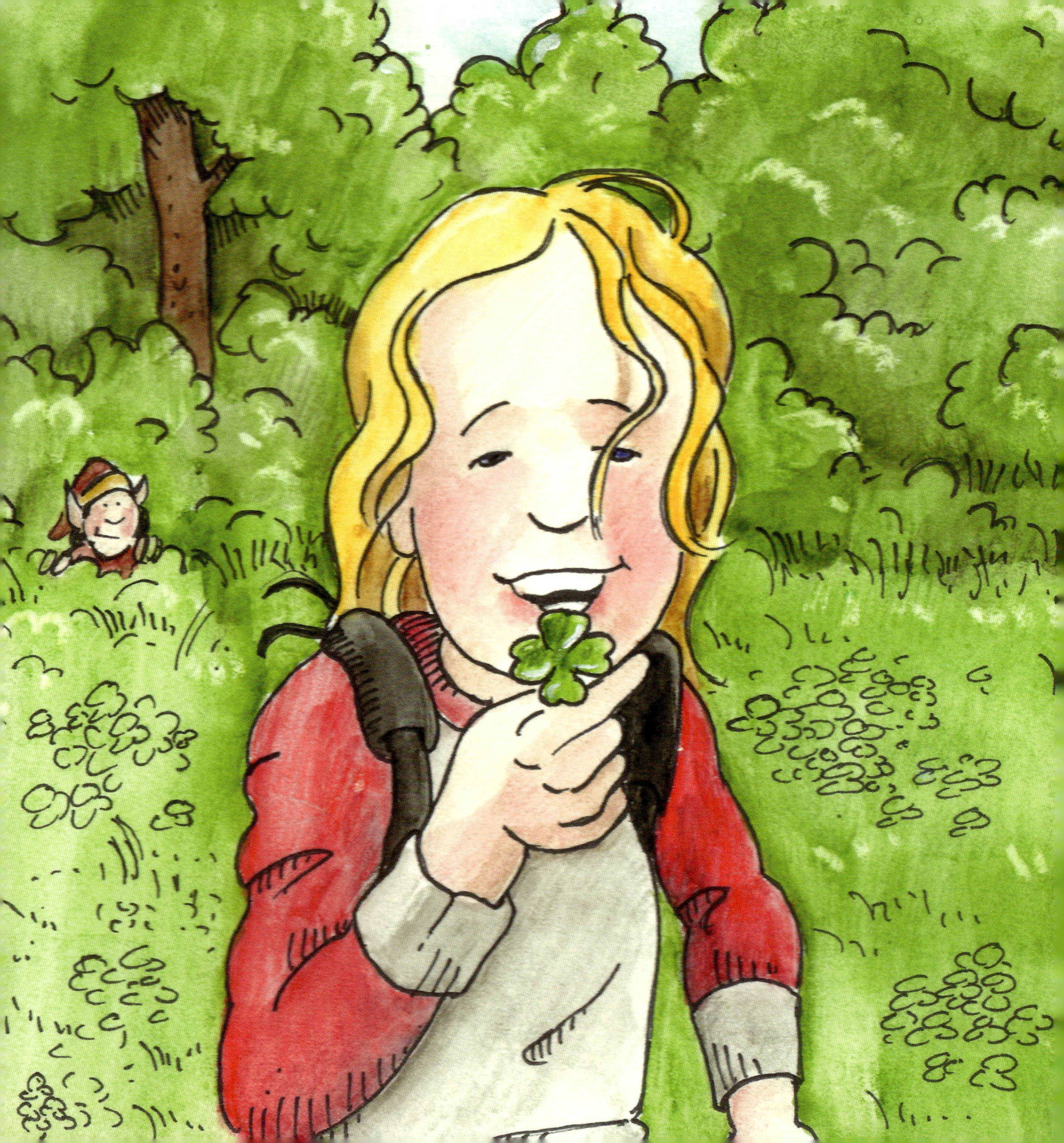

Dear _____,

How wonderful that you found a 4-leaf clover. They say that 4-leaf clovers bring us luck. Who knows if that's true or not? One way or another, they are fun to find because they just *might* bring us some good luck. Elves and fairies love to hide in 4-leaf clovers. The four leaves stand for faith, hope, love, and luck.

Here is a little poem I made up for you.

I'm needing some good luck today

Cause things are not going my way

But I'll see some changes

If my luck rearranges

Or at least that's what people say

I love you.

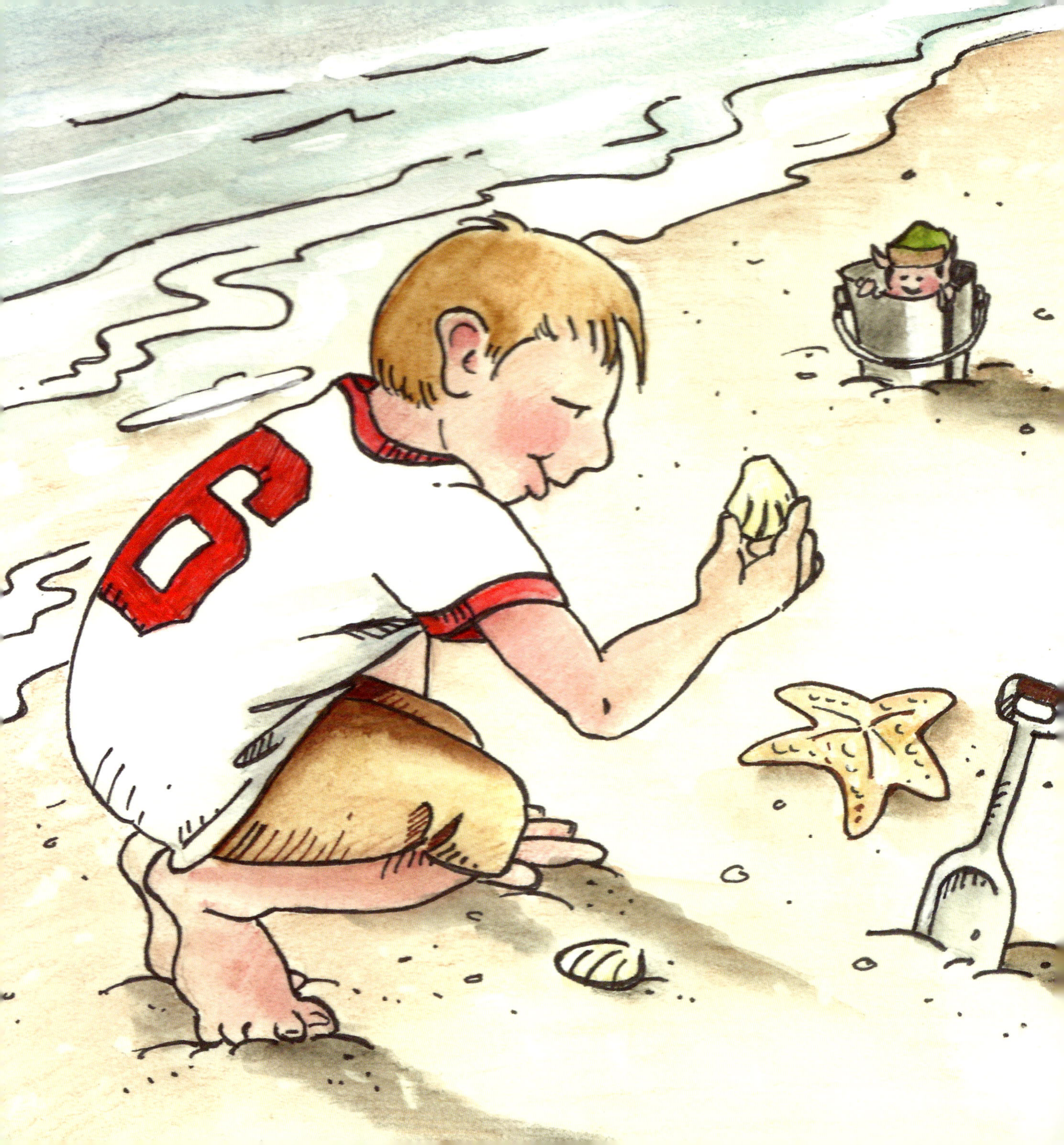
6

Dear _____,

I am glad you are discovering that there are so many hidden treasures to be found on a sandy beach. I saw you put some of them in your pocket and leave some behind for other discoverers to find. That was very thoughtful of you. I see why the shell you are holding is called a *"cat's paw."* Do you?

Here is a little poem I made up for you.

A "cat's paw" washed up on the shore
Much better than one from the store
Though I'm not sure quite how
That shell tried to "meow"
I hope you'll keep looking for more

I love you.

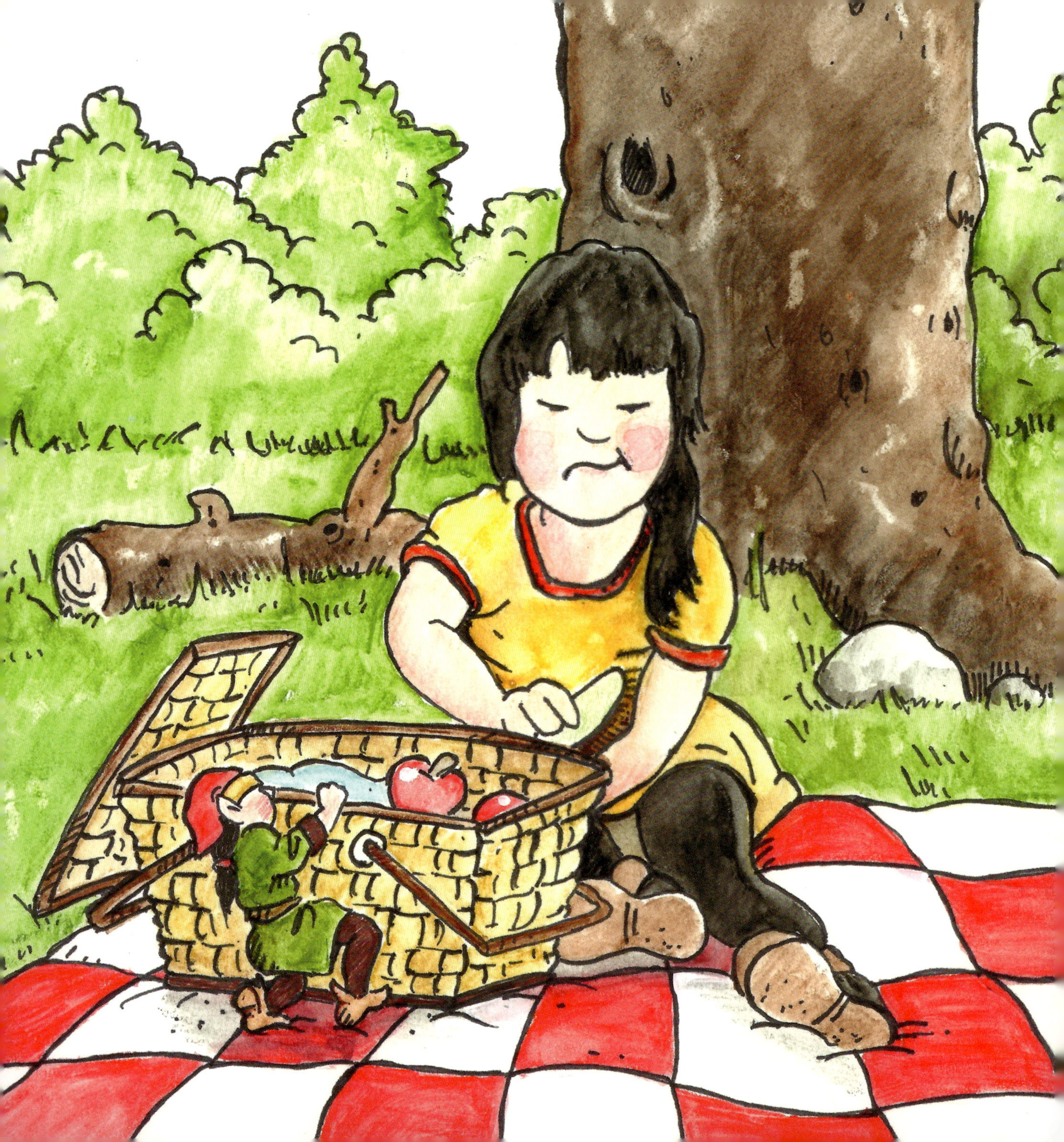

Dear _____,

I watched you pack a picnic lunch. Gummy bears and lollipops. Marshmallows and candy bars. Chips. Cookies. But then I saw your face when you opened your lunch. You saw a basketful of fruits and veggies. Beets. Brussel sprouts and avocado slices. Who packs Brussel sprouts for a picnic? I don't think it was you.

Here is a little poem I made up for you.

It's always such fun to pack lunch

To sit with a friend and to munch

When you looked at your snack

It was not what you packed

Who switched it? Do you have a hunch?

I love you.

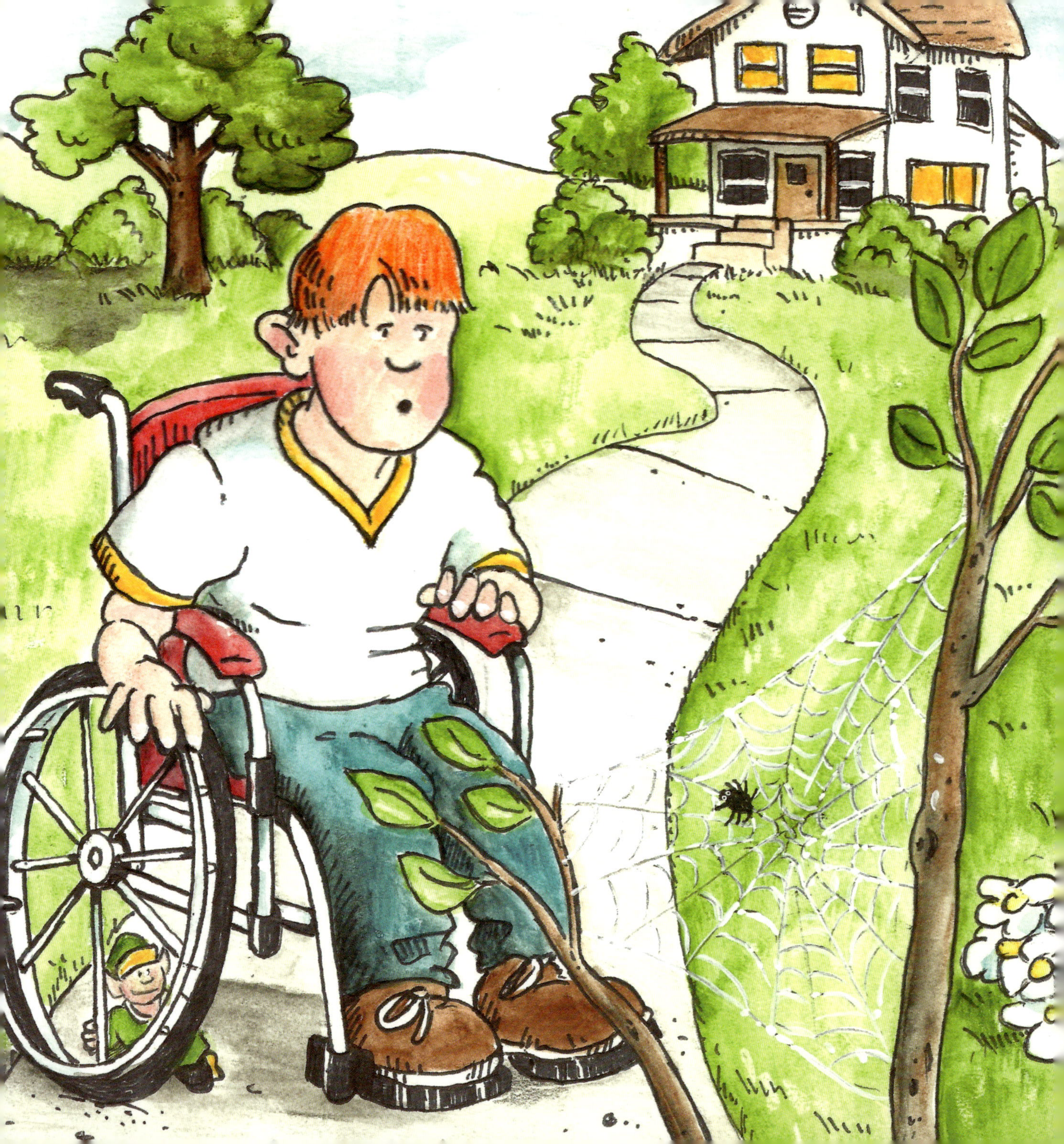

Dear _____,

I saw you investigating a spider web today. Did you know that its silk is some of the strongest material in the entire world? You were looking closely to see the design that the spider had created. Their webs are incredible works of art, aren't they? But you don't need to be afraid. Spiders can be our friends.

Here is a little poem I made up for you.

Spinning webs is truly an art

Shows spiders are really quite smart

They catch bugs for dinner

So, they are the winner

But did you know spiders can fart?

(You might want to Google this little-known fact. It is TRUE.)

I love you.

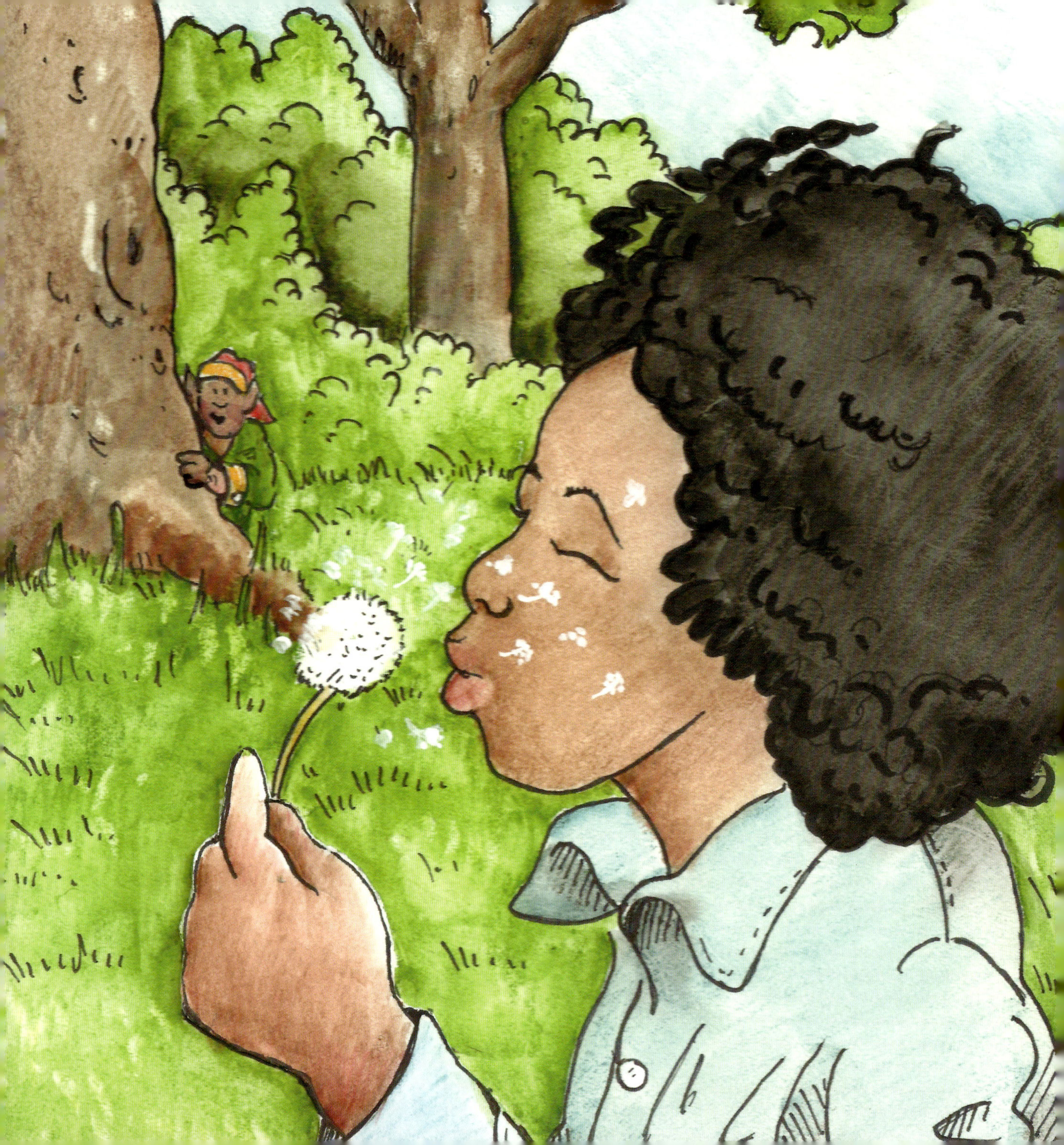

Dear _____,

I saw you pick up a fluffy dandelion today. Is it true that if you blow off every last piece of fuzz and make a wish, then your wish might come true? You took a deep breath and started to blow as hard as you could. But, a ferocious gust of wind came out of nowhere and blew all of the fluff on your face. It was funny.

Here is a little poem I made up for you.

A weed or a flower? I don't know.

But these "dandies" quickly can grow

You'll have fuzz up your nose

And all over your clothes

If the wind decides it should blow

I love you.

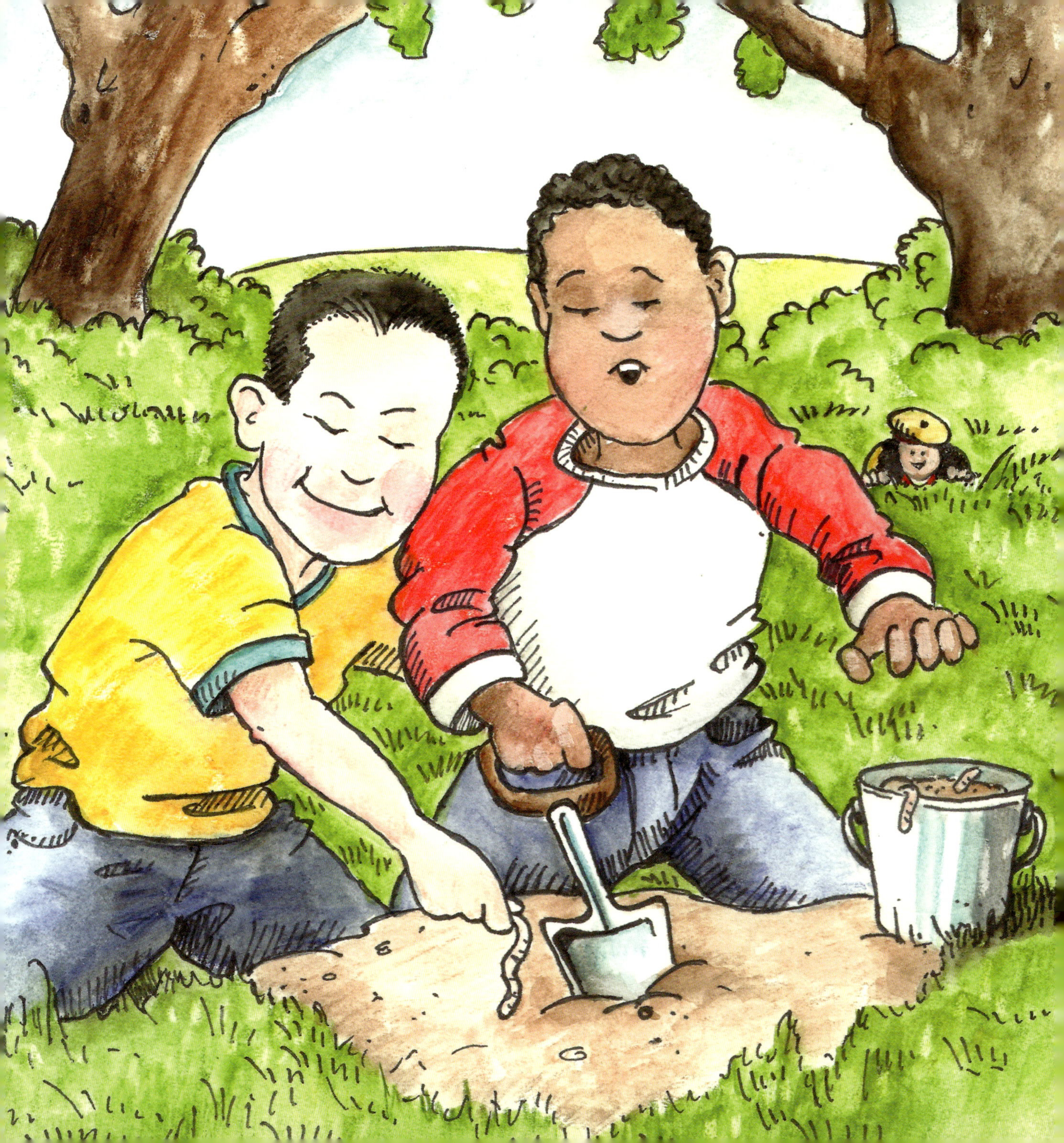

Dear _____,

Right after a beautiful spring rain, I was watching you and your friend shovel dirt trying to find enough worms to fish all day long. You knew that fish would love those worms, didn't you? But those worms were slippery and squirmy and they kept trying to get away from you. You didn't let them get away. Good job!

Here is a little poem I made up for you.

I really did not mean to snoop

When you let out a very loud whoop

But I saw that big worm

Beginning to squirm

Please don't put that worm in your soup

I love you.

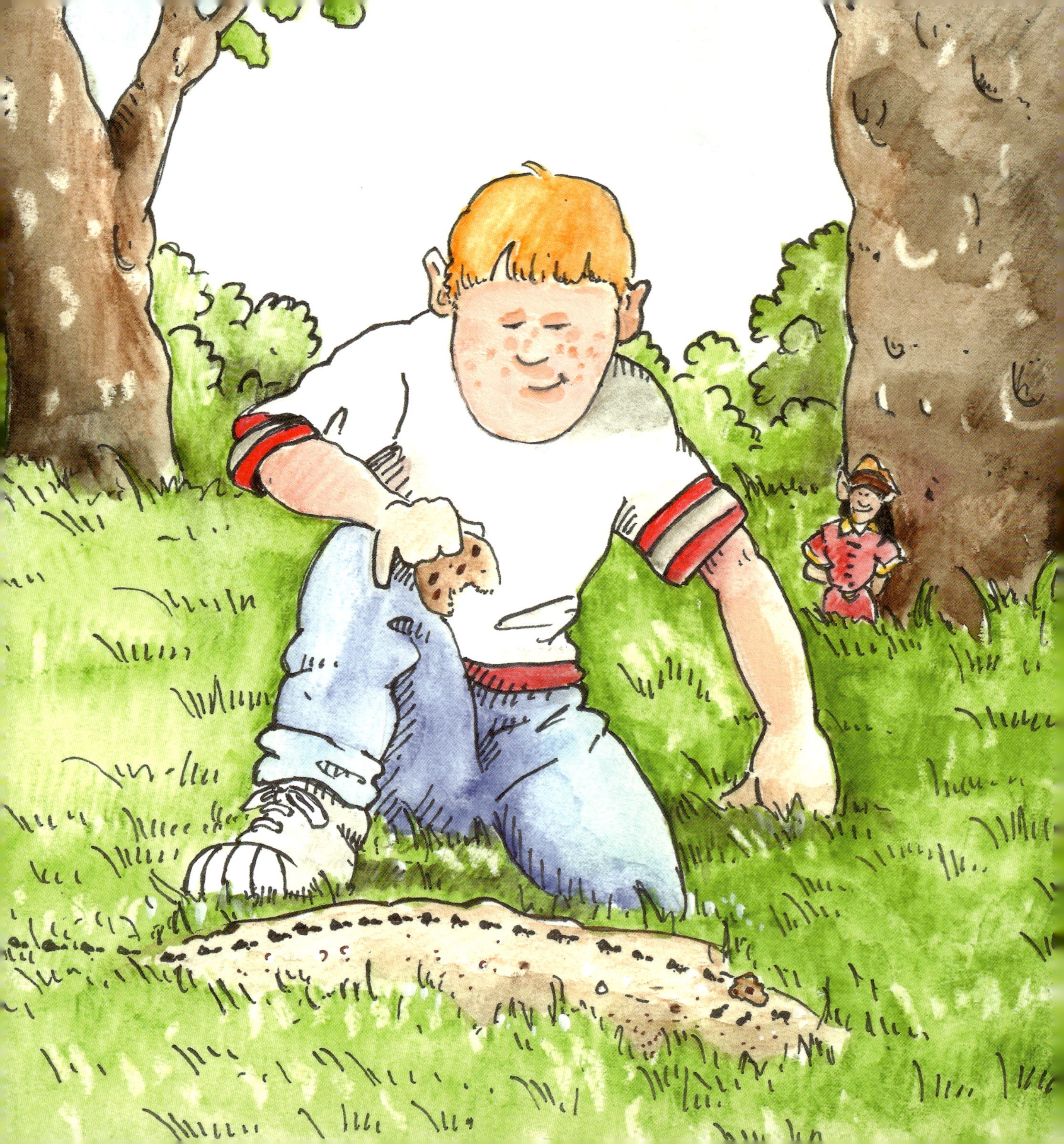

Dear _____,

I saw a parade of ants walking in such a straight line following the scent of a cookie crumb that you dropped. They nibbled away at it until every bite was gone. Then they turned around and headed to follow a new scent. Ants don't have ears but they do have 2 stomachs. Maybe that's why they like to eat a lot.

Here is a little poem I made up for you.

Though we're slightly bigger than ants
And can hide with them in the plants
We will not make you itch
And we won't make you twitch
We're better than ants in your pants

I love you.

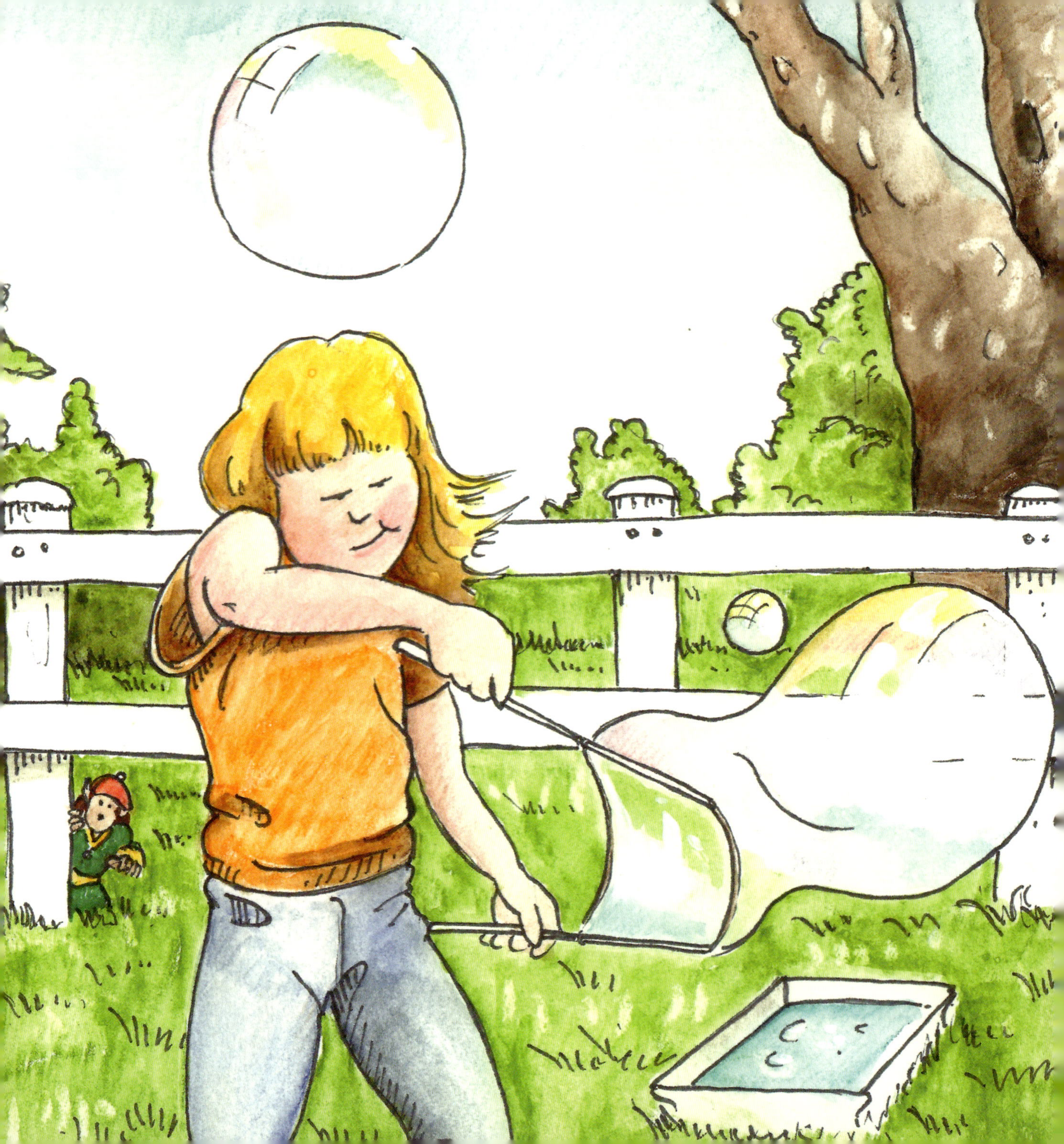

Dear _____,

I loved watching you create a special bubble solution. Playing with giant bubbles always seems like so much fun for you. We are so small that we have been known to float in the sky *inside* of a bubble, but you can't do that. I was *trying* not to laugh when a huge bubble popped on your head. But I laughed anyhow.

Here's a little poem I wrote for you.

Blowing bubbles always is fun

Especially when you can run

When one popped on your head

Your face got bright red

Good thing it was only just one

I love you.

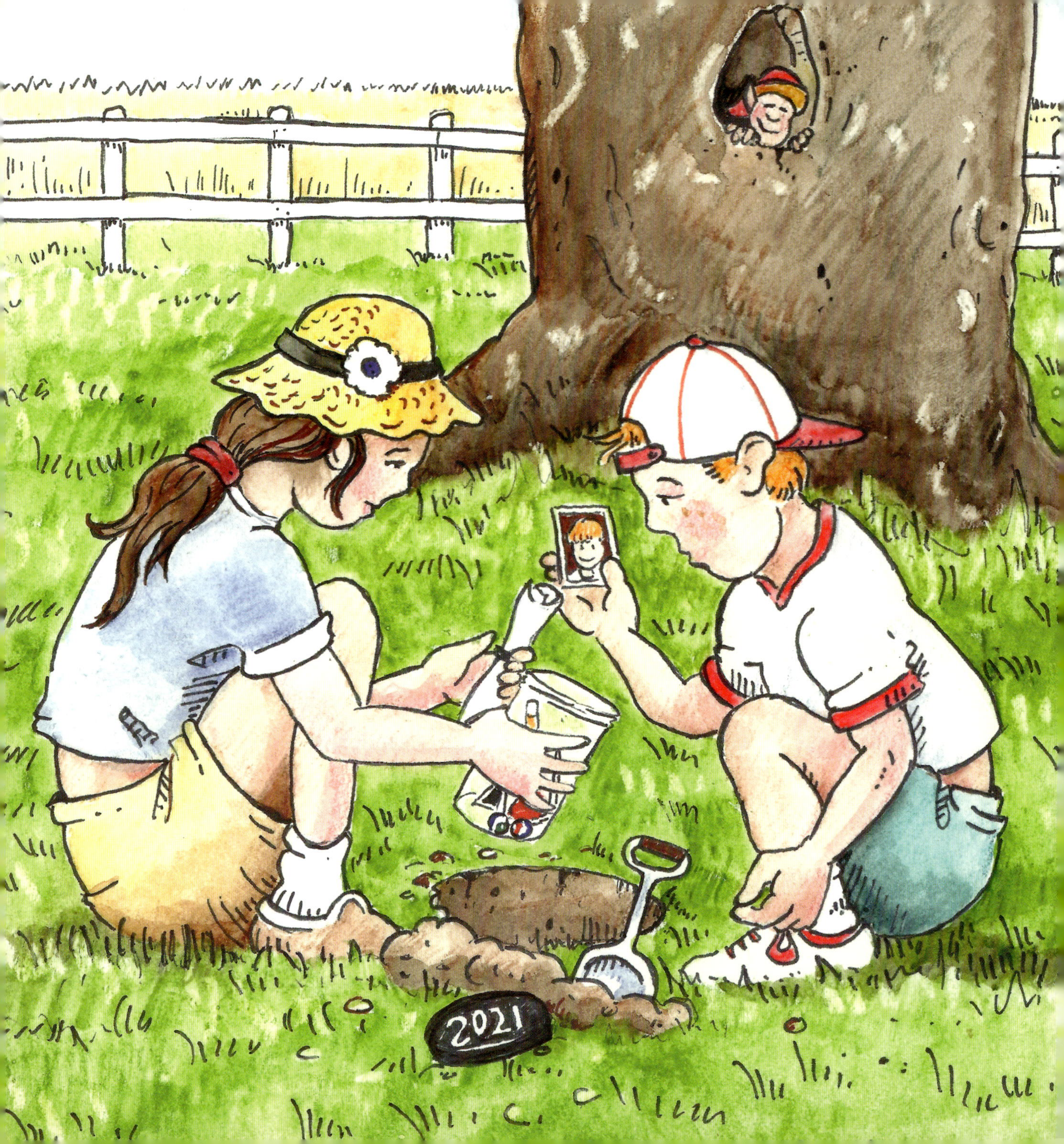
2021

Dear _____,

How creative of you to collect so many meaningful items to put in a time capsule. You searched high and low to find just the right treasures to place in the jar so carefully. Isn't it exciting to think that it might be found by someone in the future? It was nice that you put your name and the year in the jar.

Here is a little poem I made up for you.

That time capsule you made to hide

I peeked to see what was inside

If an elf had been there

I'd be saying a prayer

And then I'd have sat down and cried

I love you.

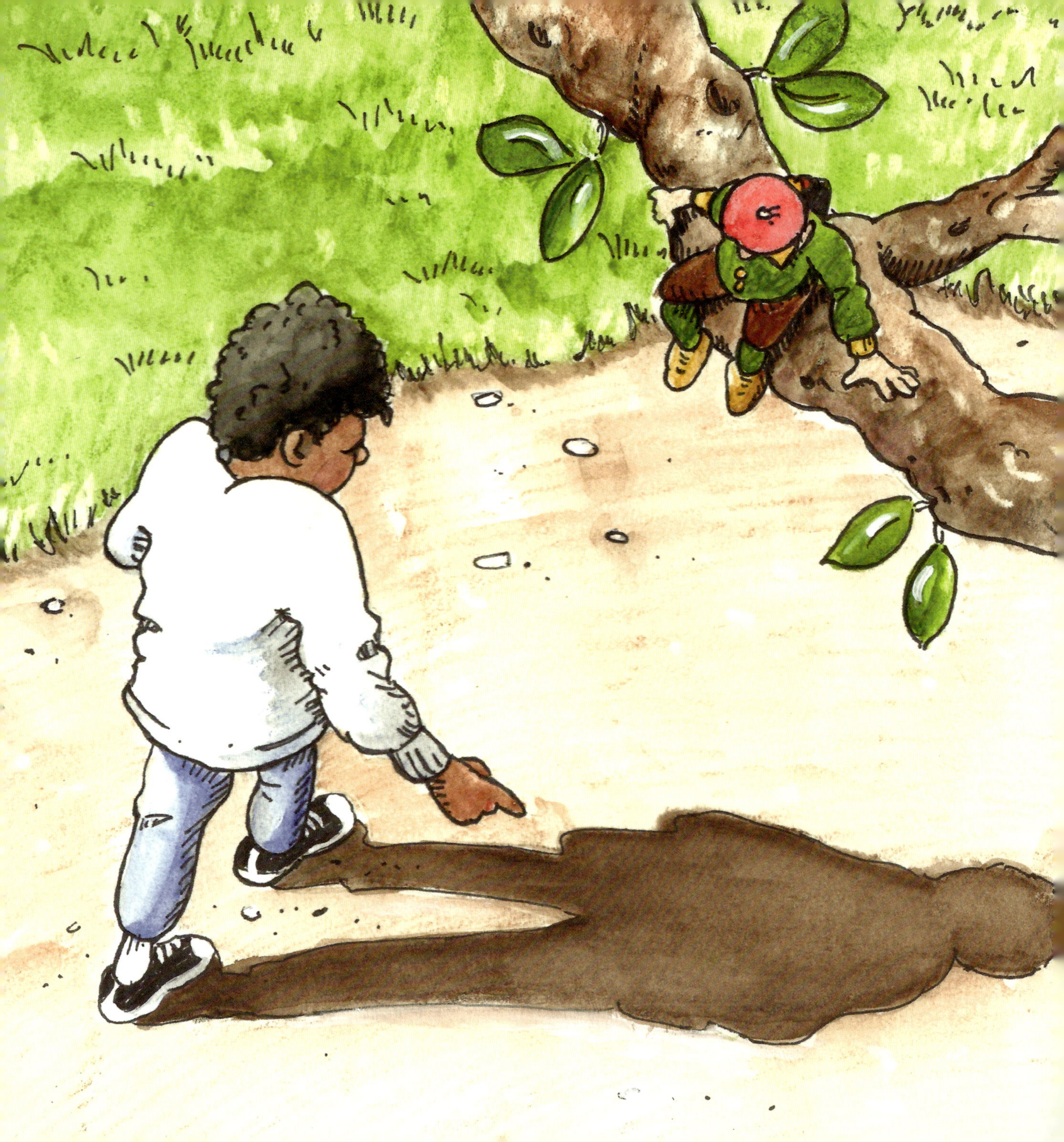

Dear _____,

It was such a bright, sunny day yesterday. I enjoyed watching you and your shadow walking down the street together. Sometimes, it looked like you were happy with him and at other times, I could tell you were not. I saw you even try to kick him away from you, but that's impossible to do, isn't it?

Here is a little poem I made up for you.

My shadow's tall, then quite tiny

Sometimes he's happy, then whiney

He thinks he's my double

Then gets me in trouble

He's really a pain in my hiney

I love you.

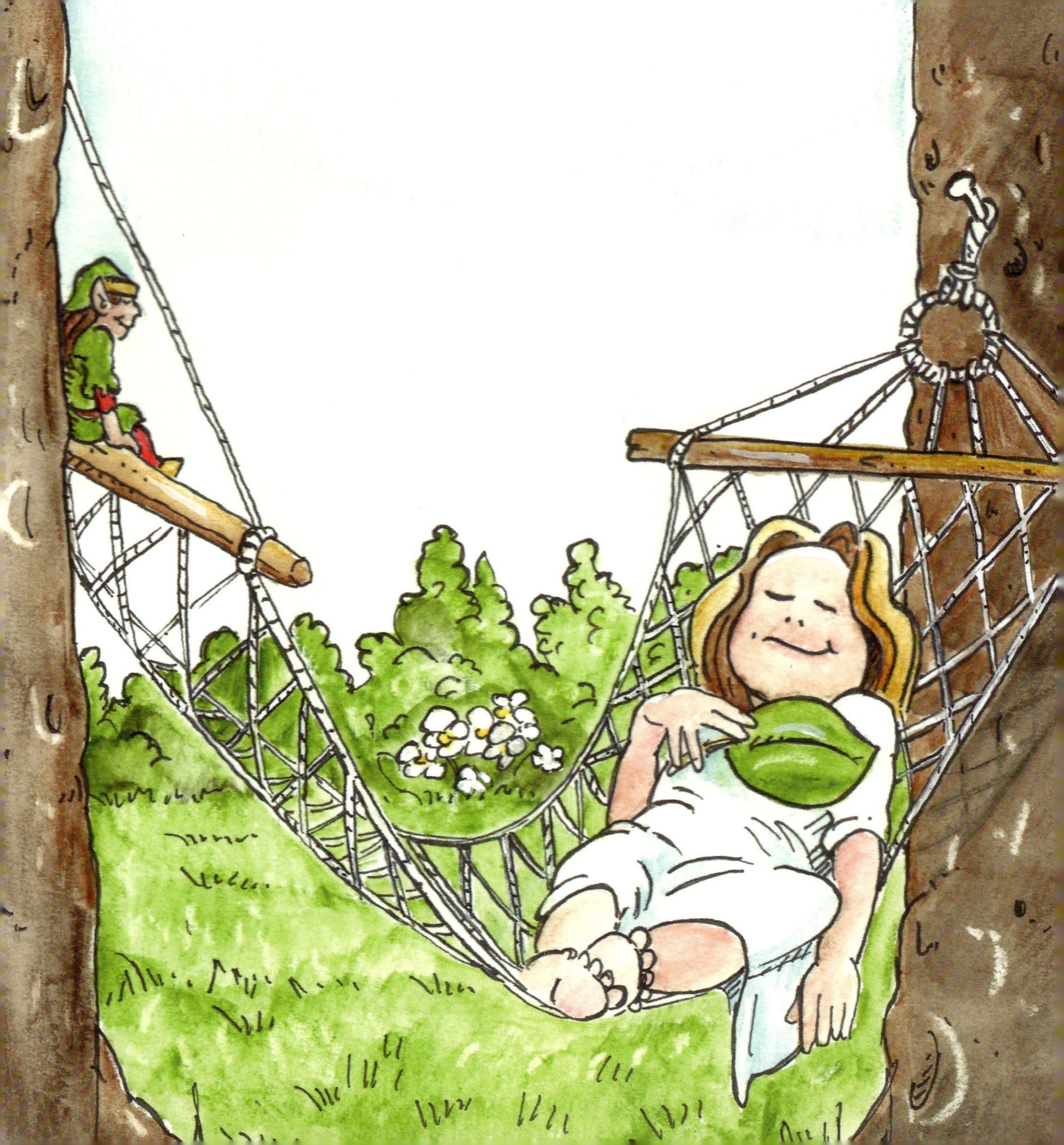

Dear _____,

I saw you enjoying a relaxing moment slowly swinging back and forth on a hammock the other day. The swaying motion put a smile on your face. Did you know that you fell asleep in the hammock? I noticed that your eyes were shut but fortunately, I did not hear you snoring like some older people in hammocks.

Here is a little poem I made up for you.

A hammock's a great place to rest

Especially if you are stressed

With your calm, peaceful smile

I knew all the while

That for friends – YOU ARE THE BEST

I love you.

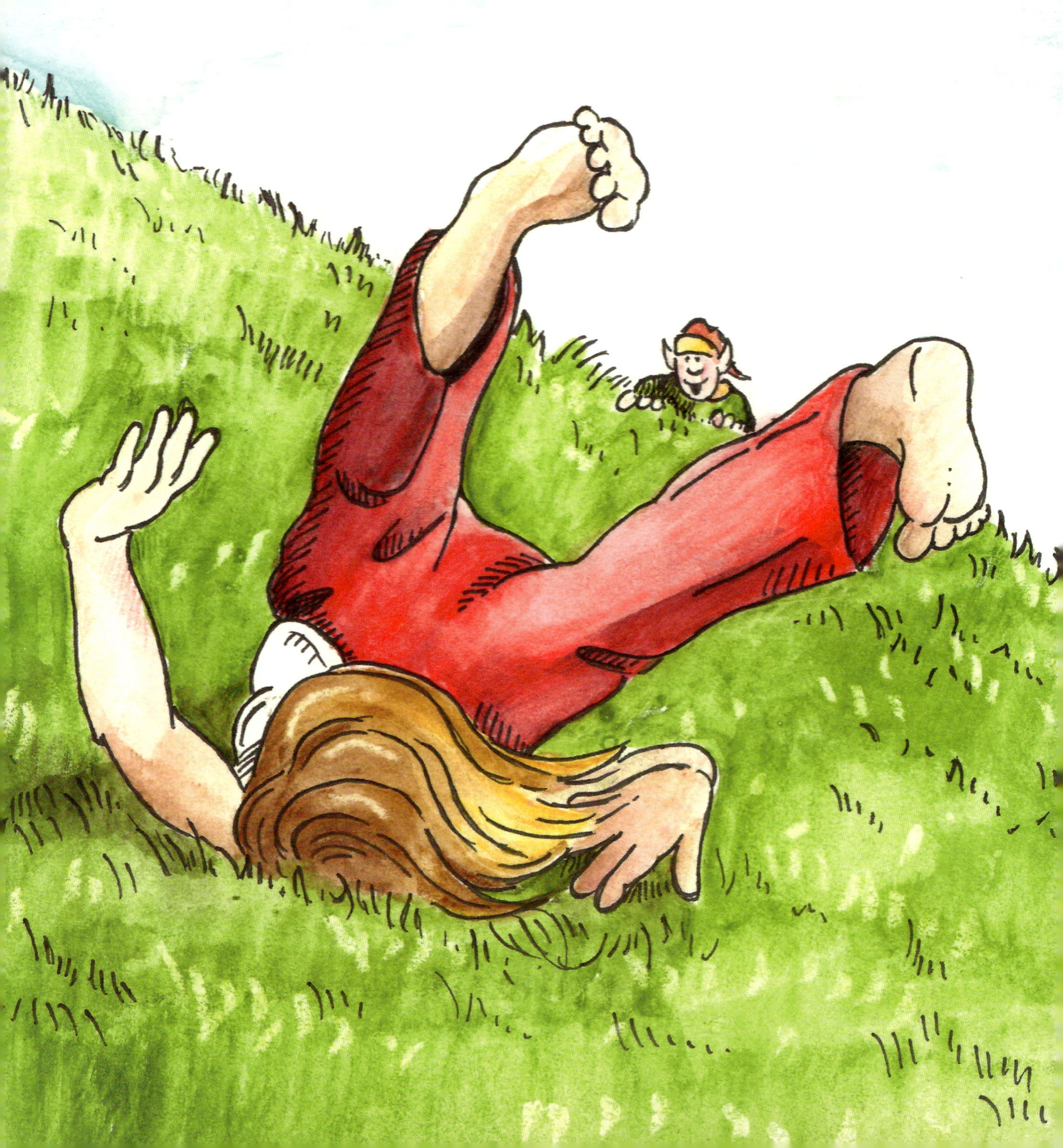

Dear _____,

I saw you rolling down a big grassy hill today. You could not stop laughing as you went flying down that hill. I saw other children join you in the fun. I even saw some 4-legged friends chasing you down the hill as well. The frog couldn't keep up with you, but the dog was trying hard to beat you. Who won?

Here is a little poem I made up for you.

A roll down the hill any place

Can become a challenging race

As you're passing a frog

Or perhaps a small dog

Be sure not to land on your face

I love you.

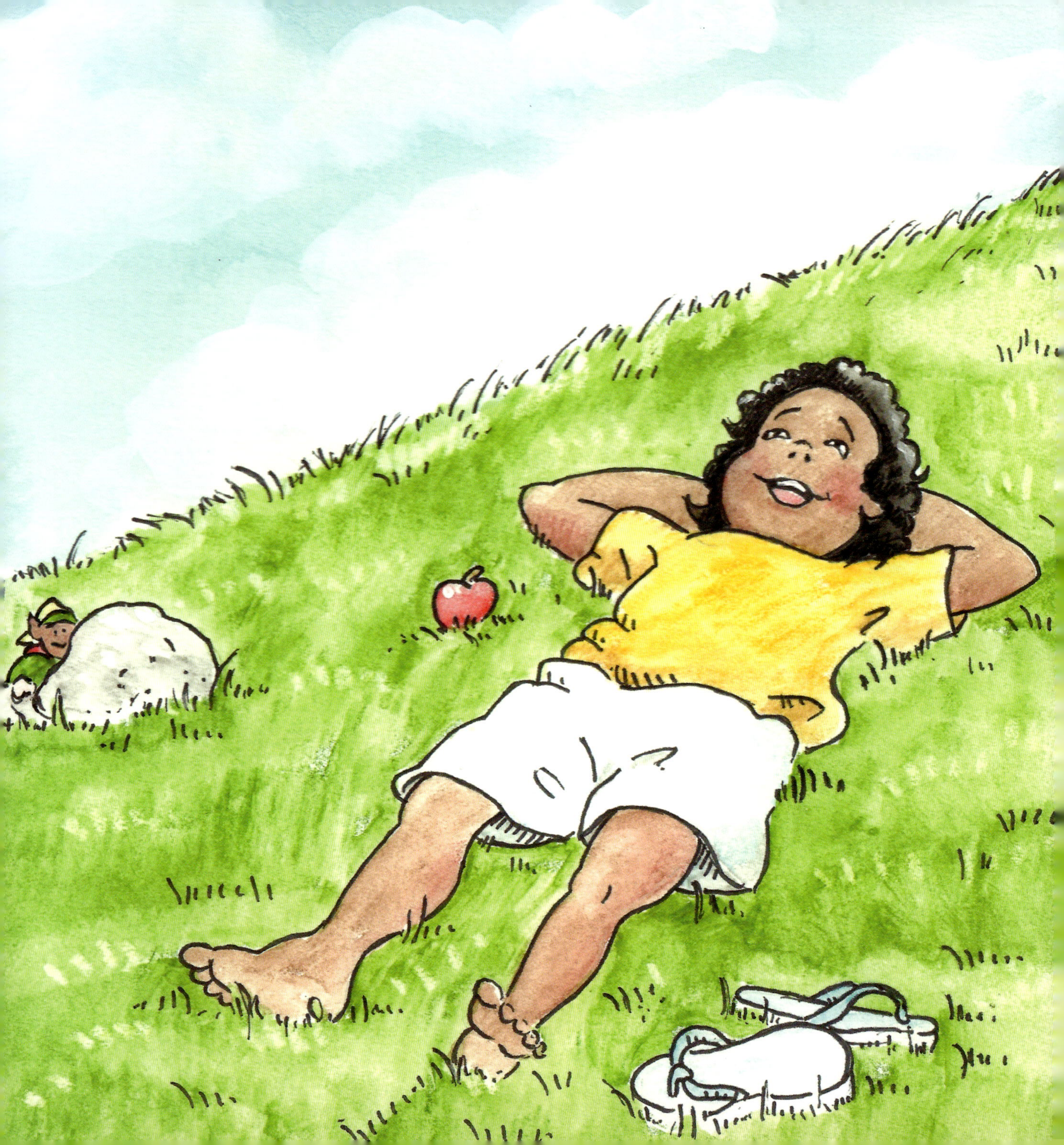

Dear _____,

I don't often get to see you so calm because you are usually on the move. It was delightful to see you just relax for a while and enjoy looking up at the clouds. Though I didn't know exactly what the clouds reminded you of, I knew they made you happy. It made me want to go lie down and look up at the sky, too.

Here is a little poem I made up for you.

I saw you watching the sky

And smile as the clouds drifted by

One cloud looked like a cat

Who was chasing a rat

He stopped. Looked at you. Winked his eye.

I love you.

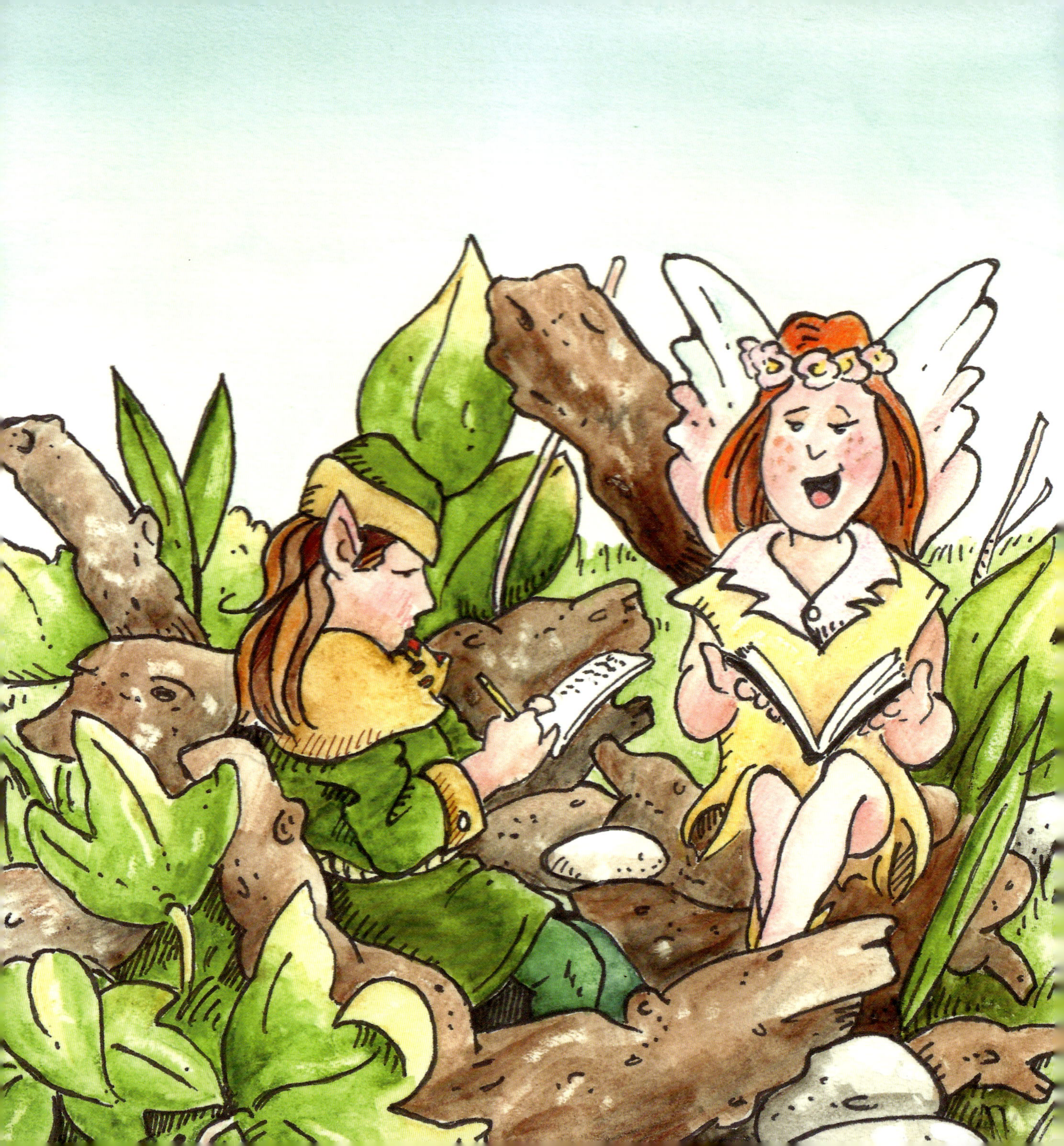

Dear _____,

I hope you are enjoying my little letters that I leave for you. It is fun finding secret places to hide your tiny letters. You seem to always find them. The letters are my way of letting you know that I am your friend. I care about you. You can always talk to me. But most importantly, I want you to know that I LOVE YOU.

Here is a little poem I made up for you.

It's important that I let you know

I'm with you — wherever you go

It's just my way to say

That I LOVE YOU each day

In the sun. In the rain. In the snow.

I love you.

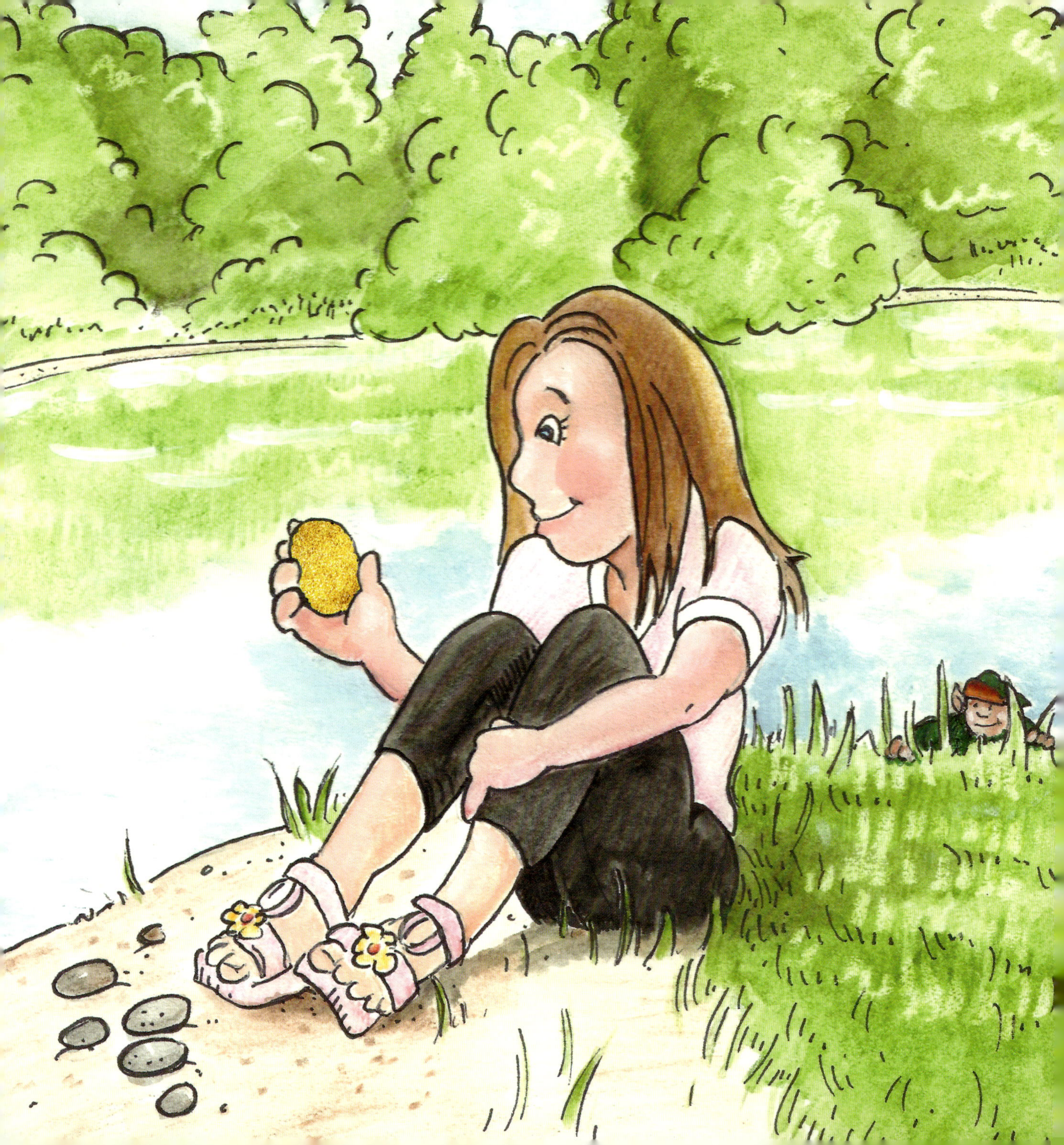

Dear _____,

You were on a mission today to find the perfect small stone for your rock collection. And you found it sparkling like gold right under your nose. Were you thinking it might hold some magic power? Or that it might be GOLD? Who knows—perhaps so? We only collect *pebbles* because our hands are so small.

Here is a little poem I made up for you.

A magical stone you have found

It sparkles like gold on the ground

You'll be rich as a queen

Before you're a teen

You'd better keep looking around

I love you.

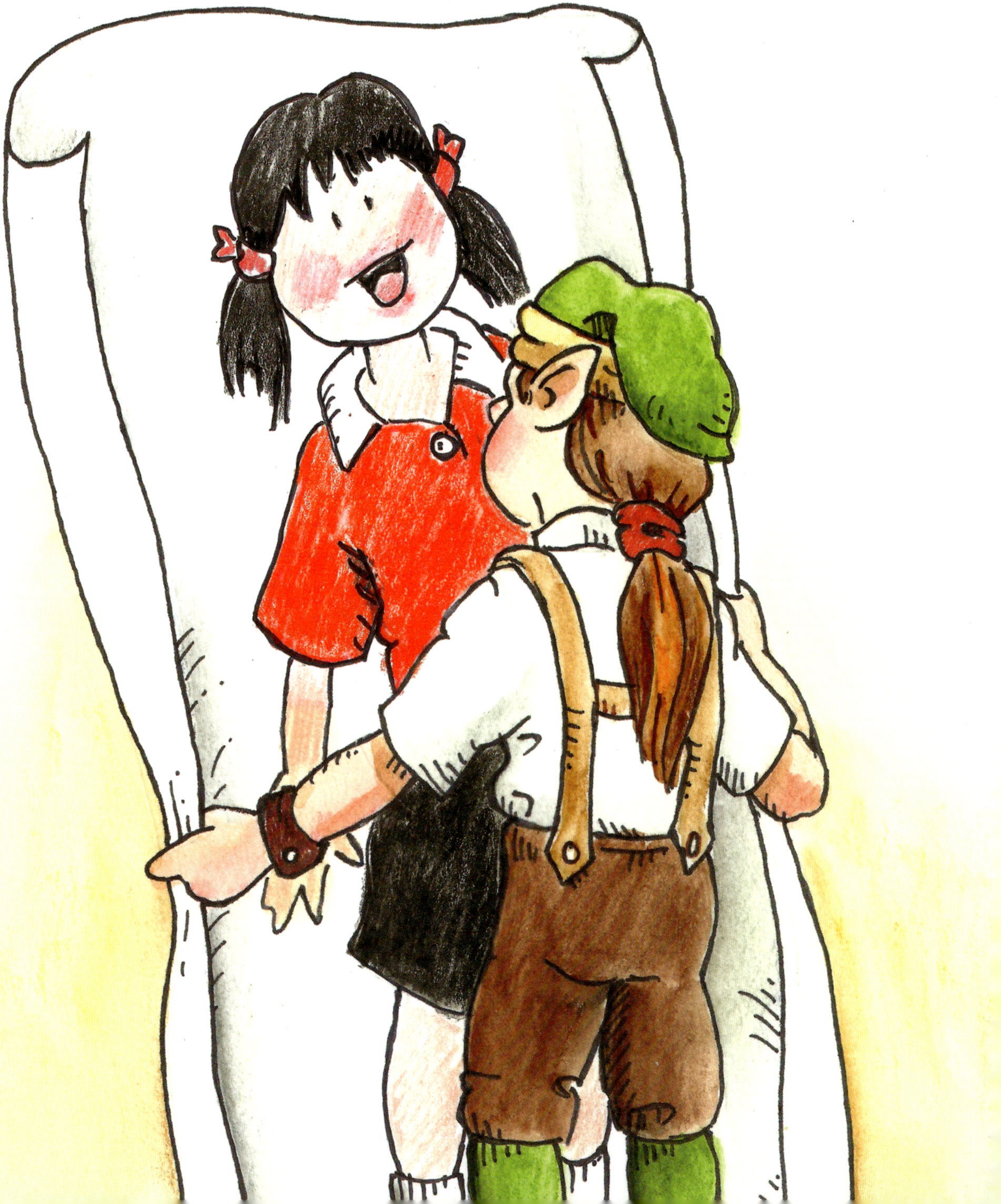

Dear _____,

That was so kind of you to leave me a beautiful picture that you had drawn of yourself so that I wouldn't forget you. How could I possibly ever forget YOU? You are ONE-OF-A-KIND. No one anywhere in the world is just like you. I will hang your picture on the wall of my home. However, there's one small problem.

Here is a little poem I made up for you.

The picture I love that you drew

Shows your head all the way to your shoe

But my home is so small

It takes up the whole wall

I truly don't know what to do

I love you.

A message from Shary, Jay & Russ

Here's a little secret we would like to share with you. Jay, Russ and I have laughed together since the creation of *The Woodland Elves*. Our friendship accelerated quickly because we were building a bridge of humor along the way. All three of us have uniquely different ways of seeing and expressing the humor in all things. It has helped us keep the stress down and our spirits up. Through life's highs and lows, we have stayed true to our purpose of PASSING THE JOY OF LIFE AROUND. We are very proud to say that we have never given up on encouraging silliness and fun. We feel it is an essential part of elf life. Joy and laughter have been a central unifying ingredient in everything we have done: books, music, card games, enchanted village, adventure trails, presentations, zoom experiences and so much more. If you would like to know anything about us, please contact Shary at 740-225-8391 or visit our website at: www.thewoodlandelves.com.

Shary Williamson (author)

Russ Kendall (I.T.)

Jay Johnston (Illustrator)